NOW YOU SEE ME

Neal Bell

BROADWAY PLAY PUBLISHING INC
224 E 62nd St, NY, NY 10065
www.broadwayplaypub.com
info@broadwayplaypub.com

NOW YOU SEE ME
© Copyright 2016 by Neal Bell

All rights reserved. This work is fully protected under the copyright laws of the United States of America. No part of this publication may be photocopied, reproduced, stored in a retrieval system, or transmitted, in any form or by any means, electronic, mechanical, recording, or otherwise, without the prior permission of the publisher. Additional copies of this play are available from the publisher.

Written permission is required for live performance of any sort. This includes readings, cuttings, scenes, and excerpts. For amateur and stock performances, please contact Broadway Play Publishing Inc. For all other rights please contact the author c/o B P P I.

First printing: June 2016
I S B N: 978-0-88145-650-9

Book design: Marie Donovan
Word processing: Microsoft Word
Typographic controls: Xerox Ventura Publisher 2.0 P E
Typeface: Palatino
Printed and bound in the U S A

NOW YOU SEE ME was first performed on 17 March 2011 at Manbites Dog Theater (Jeff Storer, Artistic Director) in Durham, North Carolina as a joint production of Manbites Dog and the Duke University Department of Theater Studies. The cast and creative contributors were:

BIXBY	Chris Burner
ACTRESS	J Evarts
CLAIRE	Rachel Klem
RAVENEL	Carl Martin
ACTOR	Tony Perucci
CAMERAMAN	Jennifer Evans
Director	Jody McAuliffe
Stage manager	Jessica McGloin
Scenic & costume design	Sonya Leigh Drum
Lighting design	Roz Fulton
Video design	William Noland
Assistant video design	Nick Wiesner
Sound design, properties	Jennifer Evans
Claire's dreams video design	Nick Wiesner

CHARACTERS & SETTING

CLAIRE, *40s*
RAVENEL, *T V producer, 50s*
BIXBY, RAVENEL's *assistant producer, 40s*

Actress, plays:
[T V], *a television set*
CLAIRE's *mother*
PATIENT #2

Actor, plays:
DOCTOR, CLAIRE's *oncologist*
CAMERAMAN
CONTESTANT #2
E R DOC
T V DIRECTOR

Offstage voices:
WOMAN, BIXBY's *girlfriend*
KILLER, *audio technician*

Time: The present

Place: New York

The set should be simple, flexible, to accommodate multiple scene changes.

Dominating the set are a number of T V screens/monitors.

Note: The character of "[T V]" is played by an actress in basic black.

When "[T V]" is presenting recaps, or previews of an episode—she can simply do the voices of the actors who would be onscreen—or she can "act out" the clips, moving when needed, to inhabit the parts.

Titles on monitors will display the names of scenes in the play, and their locations.

ACT ONE

(Title: PREVIOUSLY*)*

(The actress playing [T V] *takes center stage. Above her, a monitor comes on with the title:* PREVIOUSLY*)*

[T V]: *(As announcer:)*
Previously, on *Final Battle*...
(Pause)
Or, to be more accurate:
"Previously, in scenes that happened
before it was known who would be
on *Final Battle*..."

(Image on monitor: DOCTOR's *office)*

(Now, behind [T V], *we see* CLAIRE *and her* DOCTOR
on stage, living out the moment in the past that [T V] *is
recalling.* CLAIRE *and the* DOCTOR *mouth their lines, as* [T
V] *speaks them...or they speak their lines with* [T V].*)*

[T V]: *(As* DOCTOR*)*
We have the biopsy results.
(As CLAIRE*)*
Yes...
(As DOCTOR*)*
Claire, I'm afraid the news isn't good.
(As CLAIRE*)*
All right.
(As DOCTOR*)*
You have non-small cell lung cancer.
(As CLAIRE*)*

Non-small cell…
would that be the same as—large?
(As DOCTOR*)*
And it's aggressive.
(As CLAIRE*)*
Venti…cell, lung cancer, all right, should I—get my
affairs in order?
(As EDITOR*)*
Cut to:

(Image on monitor: A coffee shop)

(On stage, CLAIRE *is giving her* MOTHER *the news, over a
cup of coffee.)*

[T V]: *(As* CLAIRE'S MOTHER*)*
Remember your grandmother—when *she* was passing?
(As CLAIRE*)*
Who knows, momma—maybe I'll live.
(As CLAIRE'S MOTHER*)*
All that chemo and radiation.
We'd drive down the street, and clumps of her hair
would go floating out the window
(As CLAIRE*)*
I keep reading about new drugs—
(As CLAIRE'S MOTHER*)*
Are they safe?
(As CLAIRE*)*
They worked, in mice—
(As CLAIRE'S MOTHER*)*
And now you're a mouse?
(As CLAIRE*)*
I'm nothing. I'm disappearing.

([T V] *pretends to blow on a gone-to-seed dandelion.)*

[T V]: *(As* EDITOR*)*
Cut to:

(Image: The door to CLAIRE'*s apartment.)*

(On stage CLAIRE, *inside her apartment, is talking to her* EX, *through the door.)*

[T V]: *(As* CLAIRE'S EX*)*
Baby? Please open the door…
I talked to your mother—
(As CLAIRE*)*
Traitor! Go away!
(As CLAIRE'S EX*)*
You can't do this alone—
(As CLAIRE*)*
Richard, what do you want?
Do you want to be holding my head,
when I'm puking my guts out, after my chemo?
(As CLAIRE'S EX*)*
Are you doing chemo?
(As CLAIRE*)*
I haven't decided!
(As CLAIRE'S EX*)*
Then why are you puking?
(As CLAIRE*)*
Because I haven't decided!
Go—away!

(CLAIRE'S EX *is gone.)*

(Another monitor flickers to life, above and behind [T V]*.)*

(On the monitor, we get a live feed of what's happening on stage: CLAIRE *is kneeling—shaken and sweating—in front of an [unseen] toilet bowl.)*

[T V]: *(Referring to the image of* CLAIRE*)*
This would be a privileged moment.
The camera never goes into the bathroom.
(She calls out to the screen:)
Claire…

(CLAIRE, *on the screen, and on stage, looks up at the sound.)*

[T V]: *Claire…*

(CLAIRE looks around, sees no one.

CLAIRE: *(Monitor and stage)*
Is someone there?

[T V]: Just the T V, in the background.
The comfort of babble.
War, Perez Hilton, famine, Oprah...
You have to make a decision.
(Hums the theme-song to "Entertainment Tonight."

CLAIRE: *(Monitor and stage)*
But *what* decision?
What should I do?

[T V]: *(As* HOST*)*
"If you didn't think reality T V could get any stranger
than *Surviving Nugent*—that's the one where a has-
been gun-totin' rock-star gets to hunt the people who
come to his ranch—have we got a show for you..."

(On the monitor, and onstage, we see CLAIRE—*frightened
but listening.)*

(Title: EXAMINATION*)*

(Image: DOCTOR'*s office)*

*(*DOCTOR *is examining* CLAIRE, *who's wearing a hospital
gown. She's telling him about what she's heard.)*

*(From the waiting room, we hear the murmur of daytime
talk-shows.)*

DOCTOR: Deep breath. I don't watch T V—

CLAIRE: *(Breath held)*
—called *Final Battle*—

DOCTOR: And neither should you.

CLAIRE: *(Releasing breath)*
Four cancer patients—four untested new drugs...

DOCTOR: Read a book. My wife likes *War and Peace*.

CLAIRE: Do I have time for *War and Peace*?

DOCTOR: Are you a slow reader?

CLAIRE: Yes.

DOCTOR: O K, then maybe *Old Man and the Sea.*
(Pause)
It's about a fish—

CLAIRE: The fish *dies.*

(Pause)

DOCTOR: "Four new drugs." What are they?

CLAIRE: They affect the flow of blood to the tumor—

DOCTOR: *(Identifying)* "Anti-angiogenesis."
What are the names of the drugs?

CLAIRE: These are double-blind clinical trials.
So—they don't tell you what you're getting.
(Pause)
They need one more—participant.

DOCTOR: You were going to say 'contestant.'

CLAIRE: No.

DOCTOR: It *is* a game show—isn't it?

CLAIRE: They don't vote you off the island, though—
they vote you off the planet.
I'm leaving the planet anyway.
Or—I'm sorry—are *you* saving me?

(Pause)

DOCTOR: We've found three new metastases,
on your liver—

CLAIRE: Not on my brain? Because, lately—
does lung cancer go to the brain?

DOCTOR: It can…

CLAIRE: Because, lately—I've found myself—
talking to my T V set.

DOCTOR: And does it respond?

CLAIRE: Sometimes it's not even turned on—
which is fine—if it isn't speaking to me...
if it's only talking to the cancer...

DOCTOR: O K, *this* is why it's wrong—for someone to
offer you "salvation".
You're terrified—

CLAIRE: I am.

DOCTOR: So how can you possibly give your informed
consent?
It's coercion.

CLAIRE: The primary tumor's inoperable.
That leaves chemo and radiation, you said.
So I can get burned, go bald, throw up—
and "live"—no one knows for how long—
weak and in pain, in a puddle of...
or give up now—in a puddle of...

DOCTOR: Did I say "give up"?

CLAIRE: That's not what you meant?

DOCTOR: You can accept your death.
Or fight it.
Either way, you'll need all the time you can get.
Or you can *waste* that time,
while you're waiting for a miracle.

(Pause)

CLAIRE: Your bedside manner sucks.

DOCTOR: So I'm told.

CLAIRE: And you think *you're* not coercive?
(She starts to exit.)

DOCTOR: Anti-angiogenesis drugs are not "new".

(CLAIRE stops.)

DOCTOR: So you already know one thing—
that these T V people are liars.

This class of drugs has been tested before—
and the science is wrong—they don't work.

CLAIRE: Maybe this is a new generation.

DOCTOR: Maybe you never had cancer at all.
And one day soon, you'll wake up.

(On their impasse,)

(The lights change.)

(Title: COME ON DOWN!*)*

(Image: An elegant, austere office)

(On another monitor, a taped video is playing, of an anxious, frail-looking man at an interview table.)

*(*RAVENEL, *the creator of* Final Battle, *watches the nervously smiling man—*CONTESTANT 2—*who's holding out a deck of cards, to the off-camera interviewer.)*

CONTESTANT 2: *(On monitor)* Pick a card...any card...

*(*RAVENEL's *assitant,* BIXBY, *enters with a videotape.* RAVENEL *pauses the interview that was playing, to take the new tape from* BIXBY.)*

RAVENEL: I have to ask—

BIXBY: No you don't.

RAVENEL: *(Of the new D V D)* Is this one—

BIXBY: No.

RAVENEL: Let me finish: sexy?

BIXBY: She's a terminal cancer patient.
(Pause)
She's booty-licious. What do you want?

RAVENEL: You *do* know, by "sexy" I don't mean
"climb on the gurney, rip out the I Vs,
have at her—jump her jutting bones—"

BIXBY: Can evolution go backwards? You're
devolving—

RAVENEL: *Sexy*—

BIXBY: —in front of me.

RAVENEL: ...as in totally...what?
Here—warm to the touch—*alive*...

BIXBY: Not what comes to *my* mind, when I hear the words "terminal cancer patient".

RAVENEL: You are such a sensitive soul. Are you gay? She isn't "terminal" —none of them are!
(Pointing up at CONTESTANT 2, *whose frozen image is still on the screen)*
If they are, we've got no story.

BIXBY: 3-B. *Next* to terminal.

RAVENEL: There's a difference:
—"Are you in the burning building?"
—"No, I'm *next* to it."

BIXBY: What comes to *my* mind is—nothing.
"Terminal—cancer—patient."
Nothing.
"Did I leave a burner on?
Fuck, is it raining?
What should I have for lunch?"
—and by then—I'm far away from whatever it was I did not want to think about.

RAVENEL: *(Reminding)*
Terminal cancer.

BIXBY: *(Thinking)*
"Maybe a tuna on rye." See how that works?
(Pause)

RAVENEL: Do you like me, Bixby?
(Pause)
Do you?

BIXBY: No.
(Trying to qualify:)

Well, your energy—
your belief in—what you believe in…
your ferocious—
(Giving up)
no.

RAVENEL: Why not?

BIXBY: Because you can say a cancer patient is sexy
without any irony.

RAVENEL: *(Mock surprise)*
I always thought you were straight.
Guess that recruitment effort is working, huh?
(Anticipating)
"You can't fire me—I quit!"

BIXBY: Am I fired?

RAVENEL: *(Suddenly a little weary)*
Life is not that simple, my friend.

BIXBY: What do I have to do, to get fired?

RAVENEL: Stop believing in me. That's all.
And by "me" —I guess I mean "money'''

BIXBY: Is it always about the money?

(RAVENEL unfreezes the tape on the monitor.)

CONTESTANT 2: *(On monitor)* Was it the seven of hearts?

INTERVIEWER: *(O C)* Wow! That's impressive.

RAVENEL: Just play the fercochte tape.

*(BIXBY moves to change the tapes. CONTESTANT 2, on the
monitor, disappears.)*

(In his place, we now see CLAIRE at a kitchen table.)

(Title: AUDITION TAPE)

*(CLAIRE sits at a kitchen table, facing an [unseen]
camcorder.)*

(Behind her is the talking [T V].)

CLAIRE: This is my kitchen.
This is where I...
after I got the—diagnosis...
after I got in my car—
I came home, I sat down—here...
(Pause)
I guess I turned on the T V—

[T V]: No you didn't.

(CLAIRE's not surprised that the [T V] talks [and seems to be a woman].)

CLAIRE: *(Gesturing:)*
This is my T V.
(Pause)
I watch a lot of T V.

(Pause)

[T V]: I'm not your friend.

CLAIRE: —said my T V set.
I'm talking to—I find myself—
conversing with the T V. *(Gestures:)* This one.
Late at night.
It's always—late.

[T V]: I'm not your friend.

CLAIRE: No, I realize that—
(Rethinking:)
I *don't* realize that. Most things. I don't—
Or not until it's mostly too late.
"Oh—*you're* the one I should've married."
"*That's* what they mean by "suspicious mole!"

[T V]: I distract you, on occasion.

CLAIRE:—said my not-so-large, rectangular
pedestal-base flatscreen. In basic black.

[T V]: *(Ancient vaudeville joke)*
"Tickle your ass with a feather?"

CLAIRE: What?

[T V]: "Typically nasty weather?"

CLAIRE: *What?*

[T V]: "Lady, it's fuckin' freezing outside!"
I distract you. On occasion.

(CLAIRE *tries to make herself focus.*)

CLAIRE: *(To her unseen audience)*
So you can see why I'd like—
they tell me the cancer's not in my brain—yet—
but—I'm talking to my T V.
So I need to do something else, because—
I think my doctors are killing me.
(Pause)
Well, I guess I was killing *myself*, before the
doctors lent me a hand… or didn't:
Two packs a day. Too late:
"Wait—cigarettes give you cancer?"

[T V]: *(Announcer voice)*
"So ask your doctor *now*—…"

CLAIRE: About what?

([T V] *doesn't answer.*)

CLAIRE: I've heard about new drugs…

[T V]: I'm not your friend.

CLAIRE: *(Almost snapping)*
But you *are* informative.

[T V]: *(Announcer voice)*
"…—if some undeniably toxic agent
might be right for *you.*"

(Pause)

(On the monitor, we start to get a live feed of CLAIRE,
as she tapes herself.

CLAIRE: I'm always afraid. From the moment I wake.
It's difficult, to—live that way.
So—I wanted to be on your show.
(Pause)
I *want*—want *now*—to be a—contestant.
Please.
(Pause)
Please.
(Pause)
Fuck.
Cut!

(CLAIRE's image fills the screen, as she approaches the camera.)

(Image freezes, then rewinds. CLAIRE hits play.)

CLAIRE: *(On monitor)*
So—I wanted to be on your show.
(Pause)
I *want*—want *now*—to be a—contestant.
(Pause)
Please.

(CLAIRE hits "pause".)

CLAIRE: *(In person)*
"Miss Lucci, it's the Emmy Committee,
line one…"
(She rewinds, hits play.)

CLAIRE: *(On monitor)*
I *want*—want *now*—to be a contestant.

(CLAIRE presses "pause" again, then "record", then quickly moves back to her stool.)

(On the monitor, we see CLAIRE resuming her seat, facing the camera.)

CLAIRE: *(In person)*
Sorry—technical glitch.
And I don't mean, "Isn't that cute, that she

doesn't know how to operate—..."
I swear I'm *not* a Luddite!
I just do not—understand—technology.
Any of it. It's all a black box.
Like my body.
What's an M R I?
You can see inside me—with magnets?
Am I dreaming that?
Like a "televised image".
I can see it, but it's not "there"—
how do they *do* that?
Can you tell I'm afraid?
If I were dying *right* now—
well I am, but I mean, say—O K, there's a
psychopath—
and not that I'm the *only* one—
dying—sure, we all...—but O K—
he's broken into the house,
he's found me,
he's holding me up in the air,
by the neck, with one hand, these guys are
surprisingly strong—
and suddenly he skewers me to the living-room wall,
with a big sharp knife,
I'm dangling there, he looks at me—
little quizzical tilt of the head—
like an artist, regarding his work—

[T V]: You were asking a question. Weren't you?
Lordy.
Get to the end of the question.

CLAIRE: *(To whoever will see her audition tape)*
If there was a hidden camera,
and my death was being broadcast
on a big T V, on the living-room wall
right above where I'm hanging—
if you came bursting into the house—too late?—

shouting "Claire! Where are you? Claire!"—
you rounded the corner, and there we were:
me, and the television...
would you look at me?
Or would you look at my image? On the tube?
(Pause. She lights up a cigarette, takes an almost voluptuous drag.)
I think I'd look at the image.
That's why I hope I can be on your show.

(On the monitor, the image freezes: CLAIRE enjoying her cigarette.

(Title: THE HARD DECISIONS)

(BIXBY *and* RAVENEL *look at the freeze-frame image of* CLAIRE.)

BIXBY: You like her.

RAVENEL: You don't?

BIXBY: She's insane.

RAVENEL: So—wouldn't that mean that you like her?

BIXBY: Fuck you.

RAVENEL: What was the last one? Janice?
Had to play *Ride of the Valkyrie,* to get off?

BIXBY: I told you that?

RAVENEL: You'd had a few.
(Pointing to the monitor)
This one.
Something about her.

BIXBY: Like how she wants in, to a clinical trial,
to test a promising lung-cancer drug,
while French-inhaling a cigarette?

(Pause)

RAVENEL: Remember when everyone smoked?

BIXBY: You weren't even born.

RAVENEL: I miss it anyway.
I look good in a tux.
And she's wearing a strapless gown—whoever she is,
at the time—
we're standing on a terrace,
all the lights of the city below us...
She says, "May I have a light?"
And I know that means I am going to fuck her.

(BIXBY *indicates the frozen image of* CLAIRE.)

BIXBY: *(A question)* Fuck *her...*

RAVENEL: Something about her...

BIXBY: You don't get to play with this one.

RAVENEL: No?

(BIXBY *starts to exit.*)

BIXBY: I'm deleting her contact info.

RAVENEL: You're fired.

BIXBY: *(Hesitant)*
You can't fire me—I quit.

RAVENEL: *(Of* BIXBY's *line)*
Just not believable, right?
You don't even make a move for the door.

(Pause)

BIXBY: I have an old picture, of my parents...
at a cocktail party, Newport Beach...
on a balcony overlooking the Pacific...
smoking like chimneys...

RAVENEL: They were beautiful.

BIXBY: How do *you* know?

RAVENEL: You showed me that picture.

BIXBY: I did?

RAVENEL: You'd had a few.

(Brief pause)

BIXBY: Do I drink too much?

RAVENEL: Or not enough. Are you numb?

BIXBY: No.

RAVENEL: Then not enough.

(RAVENEL reverses the tape, to the moment when CLAIRE lights up again.)

RAVENEL: And this final cigarette? C'mon:
You never had break-up sex?

BIXBY: "You can't leave me, I'm leaving *you*?"

RAVENEL: And then you try to annihilate each other—
one last time.

CLAIRE: *(On the monitor)*
That's why I hope I can be on your show.

(BIXBY and RAVENEL watch CLAIRE smoking.)

BIXBY: She talks to her T V set, Ravenel.
And it answers her. They converse.

RAVENEL: And if she cracks up, on camera—mid-season—
just how cool will *that* be?
—if she rips apart at the seams and we capture
every jibbering scream and
every glistening string of drool…

(Title: GETTING TO "YES")

(CLAIRE stumbles into her apartment, juggling keys, a bag of groceries, and her cell-phone ringing away in her purse.)

(The [T V] *is on.)*

[T V]: *(As* LATE-NIGHT HOST*)*
So they're planning this new reality show—about
dying people.
Hey, *I'm* there!

(Canned laughter.)
Dying people are funny…

(As the LATE-NIGHT HOST *is waiting for the laffs to subside,* CLAIRE *finally snags her cell-phone.)*

CLAIRE: Hello?

[T V]: *(As* LATE-NIGHT HOST*)*
I'm watching T V last night, with my wife,
there's a knock at the door, she answers it.
This network suit is standing there, apologetic,
says to my wife—
"We understand you're dying…"
She leaves him at the door, settles back down on the couch,
she goes, "It's for you."
(More canned laughter)
I know, right?

CLAIRE: *(Into phone)*
All right, I'll be there.
Thank you.
Thank you very much.

[T V]: *(As* LATE-NIGHT HOST*)*
I mean, seriously—who would do this?

CLAIRE: *(To* [T V]*)*
I'm in.
Ohmygod, they want me to do an interview.
(Pause)
I'm *in*!
(She starts to cry.)

[T V]: *(As* LATE-NIGHT HOST*)*
"—Doctor, it hurts when I go like this…"
(Makes a wing-flapping motion)
—So don't go like *this*…"
(Dropping the imitation)
—When I go like this, I mean, and no one's watching…

when I'm all alone...
when it's four o'clock in the morning,
and the pain is so bad—
like I'd backed up onto a rusted spike
and I couldn't pull myself off it—
if someone were there, to hold me...
to stop me from going like this...
(She flaps her arm, like a broken wing, starts crying too, like
CLAIRE.*)*

(Unnerved by something, CLAIRE *looks up at [T V], sees a*
kind of reflection of herself.)

(Title: INTERVIEW)

*(*BIXBY *and* RAVENEL—*off an elaborate questionnaire—are*
grilling CLAIRE.*)*

(A CAMERAMAN *to one side is shooting the interview. On a*
monitor: a live feed of the scene we're watching.)

RAVENEL: Divorced—when?

CLAIRE: Two years ago.

BIXBY: Amicably?

CLAIRE: Is that possible?

BIXBY:	RAVENEL:
No.	Yes.

(Pause)

RAVENEL: *(Looks at his notes)*
Your ex—Richard—

CLAIRE: Or, as I called him—*Dick.*

RAVENEL: Has he been supportive?

CLAIRE: You mean, does my dying make him like me
more?

*(*BIXBY *makes a note,* CLAIRE *sees him.)*

CLAIRE: You have a checklist.

BIXBY: *(Vague)*
Basic—traits…

(CLAIRE *makes a pretend "check" in the air.*)

CLAIRE: "Bitch."

BIXBY: *(Correcting)*
"Dark."

CLAIRE: Is that bad?

RAVENEL: Nothing is good or bad, to us.

CLAIRE: Nothing?

RAVENEL: Nada. With a show like this, it's all about the mix.
(Pause)
Do you have a boyfriend?

CLAIRE: No.

RAVENEL: Casual sex with anyone?

CLAIRE: Not since—…no.

(CLAIRE *sees* BIXBY *making a check, makes air check-marks of her own.*)

CLAIRE: "Frigid."
(Rethinks, to check a more accurate quality)
"Puritanical."
(Rethinks)
"Not horned up, in face of approaching death."

RAVENEL: Not since when, Miss Forster?

(The CAMERAMAN *moves in, to get* CLAIRE's *reaction. She clams up.)*

(CLAIRE's *face appears in close-up, on the Monitors.*)

BIXBY: Forget about the camera.

CLAIRE: *("Yeah, right")*
Forget about the man rubbing up against you,
on the subway…

CAMERAMAN: Was not me.

(RAVENEL *glares at the* CAMERAMAN.)

CAMERAMAN: Just sayin'…

CLAIRE: My ex came over, one night…
I don't know, a few months ago, I guess it was.
He said I still had some books of his.
It was hot that day, he was sweating,
and I'd always liked the way he smelled…
and it just—played out. It was stupid.
He fell asleep right after, like he always did –
I just lay there…
I thought maybe I'd pulled a muscle, something –
that's the first night I felt it.
A little pain in the back,
from getting too jiggy with my ex…

(*Pause*)

RAVENEL: And not since then…

CLAIRE: No.
Unless you count the man in the subway.

(RAVENEL *signals the* CAMERAMAN *to stop.*)

RAVENEL: O K. I think we have enough.

(*The monitors all go blank.*)

CLAIRE: (*"Sally Field"*)
"You like me. You *really* like me."
Sorry.
"Don't call me—I'll blah, blah, blah…"

RAVENEL: (*Ignoring her awkwardness*)
One final thing, Miss Forster—
If you wouldn't mind taking a look at a short
dramatic re-enactment—
written by my colleague here,
the redoubtable Mister Bixby—

based on your application, when you describe how it felt—

CLAIRE: How—what??

RAVENEL: To receive your diagnosis.

CLAIRE: Isn't this a reality show?
Do you *need* a dramatic re-enactment?

RAVENEL: We do! Because no one was there.

CLAIRE: *I* was there! The quack of a doctor was there!

RAVENEL: And who was watching you?

(Pause)

CLAIRE: "If a tree falls in a forest—"

RAVENEL: Right.

CLAIRE: There's a sound. Because it fell on *me*.

RAVENEL: So *you* understand the context.
But does the audience?

CLAIRE: There was no audience!

RAVENEL: Now there is. And this moment is key—
when you get the diagnosis.

(Reluctantly, CLAIRE gives in. RAVENEL starts a tape.)

(On the monitor, an ACTRESS and an ACTOR, playing CLAIRE and her oncologist.)

ACTRESS: So give it to me straight, doc—

CLAIRE: Wait!

ACTRESS: How much time have I got?

CLAIRE: Can you freeze it?

(RAVENEL pauses the tape.)

BIXBY: It's not verbatim, I know—

CLAIRE: It's a crappy old movie. I'm the "brassy dame"?

BIXBY: I didn't want you to be just a mouse, in a trap.

CLAIRE: But that's what happened!
(She makes the sound of a mouse-trap springing)
Thwack!
(Pause)
I sat down, the doctor met my eye,
he said, "I'm afraid I have bad news".
And then the room got very hot. And loud. And very
still.
Like, "Whoa—there's a big hunk of cheese in my
paws!" —like, "Fuck, did I just make a mistake?'—
and then *THWACK!*
That's what happened.
I did not say, "Nuts to you, warden".
Or, "Give it to me straight, doc".
(She is fighting not to cry.)
I did *not* say, "Nothing is good or bad."
The pain is bad.
I don't walk very well…

(RAVENEL starts the D V D again.)

CLAIRE: I wanted him
to die.
Can I say that?

ACTRESS: So give it to me
straight, doc: how much
time have I got?

ACTOR: How much do
you need?

ACTRESS:

BIXBY:
(Rattled)
Did you mention that,
on your application…?

Thirty—forty—years?

ACTOR:
I don't like to talk about
odds. You get into
averages. And who's

CLAIRE:
(Over the video)

I wanted this—crab to be growing inside him. Waving its claws around in the dark. average? Eight out of ten could be dead in a year. And you could be Number Nine.

(RAVENEL pauses the D V D again, to hear CLAIRE better.)

CLAIRE: I wanted to see
it come out.
Through his chest.
(Ripping sound)
DOOJSH!
(She mimes the chest-busting moment from Alien, *using her fist for the baby monster—poking its head out the ruptured chest, looking around, then scooting away.)*

(To provoke CLAIRE, RAVENEL starts the D V D again.)

ACTRESS: Eight out of ten…

ACTOR: It's a numbers game.
I don't like to throw around
numbers.

(CLAIRE grabs the remote from RAVENEL, hits pause.)

BIXBY: I thought, from your application, he was
trying to give you hope.

CLAIRE: "Doojsh!"

BIXBY: Offering, at least the possibility.

CLAIRE: I—don't—*want*—it!

RAVENEL: Then why are you trying out for our show,
Miss Forster?
Don't you want to live?

CLAIRE: I want to live without hope.

BIXBY: I don't think that's possible.
Is it?

(Pause)

CLAIRE: Wanta find out?
Then let me be a contestant on your show.

RAVENEL: *(Quietly, to himself)*
Thwack.

(Title: VALKYRIE*)*

(Image: BIXBY's *apartment)*

(A monitor is showing a late-night talk-show, without sound.)

(We hear, offstage, the cries of a woman approaching orgasm.)

(The cries climax.)

(A moment later, we hear a door open.)

(Wagner's Ride of the Valkyrie *blares out, then fades as the door closes.)*

*(*BIXBY, *in a bathrobe, wanders in.)*

(He stares at the late-night show on T V.)

(Then he clicks a remote, turning on a video player.)

(It's CLAIRE—*in the audition-tape she made.)*

*(*BIXBY *watches the silent images.)*

(As he does, [T V] *appears. She speaks the words of the silent* CLAIRE—*part of the tape we hadn't heard before.)*

[T V]: *(Speaking as* CLAIRE*)*
It started with a pain in my back…
of course, you imagine "cancer" —well, maybe not
you—
I'm a hypochondriac…
You're afraid of seeing a doctor,
so you tell yourself—"pulled muscle"—
your drag yourself through a couple of months…
but it didn't get better, I couldn't sleep—
then they finally did a biopsy—and, it *was* cancer.
Like—surprise! Even hypochondriacs…

WOMAN: *(From offstage bedroom)*
Bix?

BIXBY: *(Startled)*
Yeah! Coming…

(As he hits the remote, [T V] vanishes.)

(And the monitor goes to black.)

(Title: BAD ONE)

(Image: CLAIRE's apartment)

(The DIRECTOR is attaching a mic to CLAIRE. She's started using a cane.)

DIRECTOR: You wear the mic at all times.

CLAIRE: O K…

DIRECTOR: Now give us a level. Say something.

CLAIRE: "Something." Sorry. I'm a little—
the pain is not—

DIRECTOR: *(Yelling to someone offstage)*
Killer, are we good?

KILLER *(Off)*
We're good.

CLAIRE: "Killer?"

DIRECTOR: Audio guy. Pussycat.

CLAIRE: And the cameras are…

DIRECTOR: Everywhere. Forget 'em.

CLAIRE: In the bathroom?

DIRECTOR: Yup, a Tony Perkins *Psycho*-cam.
No, not in the john.

(CLAIRE looks around.)

DIRECTOR: Don't look for them!

CLAIRE: O K, but if I stumble on one—

DIRECTOR: Never look at it.
Don't play to it.
Just live your life.
Is the whole idea.

CLAIRE: "My life". So this would be a short.
And when there's an actual *person*, with a camera—

DIRECTOR: *Never* talk to him.

CLAIRE: Not even "hello"?

DIRECTOR: "Hello" is fine. "Your fly is open…"

CAMERAMAN: *(Offstage)*
Wasn't me.

CLAIRE: "Typically nasty weather…"

DIRECTOR: What?

CLAIRE: Nothing. Sorry.

DIRECTOR: Word of advice: stop apologizing.

CLAIRE: Sorry. I mean—

DIRECTOR: We'll edit it out. But we've already got a "nice" one.

CLAIRE: Another—participant…

DIRECTOR: Yeah. Long suffering, with a smile.
He creeps me out, but what the hey.

CLAIRE: If he's the 'nice' one—what am I?

DIRECTOR: Dunno. Do you?

CLAIRE: I don't. No.

DIRECTOR: I guess we can figure that out in the editing room.

(CLAIRE *cries out, hit with a spasm of pain.*)

CLAIRE: *Fuck…*

DIRECTOR: You O K?

CLAIRE: Yeah. It's just—sometimes—
the pain is…bad.
(She stoops over, hands on knees, trying to get her breath.)

DIRECTOR: Right. You have meds for that?

CLAIRE: Oxycontin.

DIRECTOR: Sweet.
(Into headphone-set)
Are you picking this up?
(To CLAIRE:*)*
Hold on…

*(*CAMERAMAN *enters, moving in for a close-up of* CLAIRE.*)*

(Her face in pain fills up a monitor.)

*(*CLAIRE *looks at the intruding* CAMERAMAN.*)*

DIRECTOR: Remember what I said…

(Remembering, CLAIRE *looks away, still almost doubled up in pain.)*

CLAIRE: *(Through gritted teeth)*
I'm not looking—at the cameraman—
you fucking—*twat.*

(Nobody moves. The camera keeps recording.)

CLAIRE: I can be—the *bad* one…

(The DIRECTOR *nods, satisfied.)*

(Title: LOVE INTEREST*)*

(Image: RAVENEL's *office.)*

(On a monitor: Live feed of DIRECTOR *walking* CLAIRE *through her wired apartment.)*

(Continuous. BIXBY *and* RAVENEL *are watching the monitor.)*

RAVENEL: But bad with who?

BIXBY: What do you mean?

RAVENEL: I got us a night-vision camera.
Do you know what that sucker cost?
So we'd better be shooting something more
than eight hours of her sawing wood.

BIXBY: She isn't seeing anyone.

RAVENEL: I know. That's a problem. Fix it.

(Pause)

BIXBY: Any suggestions?

RAVENEL: Jed? The intern?

BIXBY: Jed is eighteen.

RAVENEL: And he's hung like a horse.

(Off BIXBY's *raised eyebrow:)*

RAVENEL: See, I'm *not* a faggot, I can look.

BIXBY: I'm not fixing up Ms Forster with an eighteen-
year-old palomino.

RAVENEL: Fine. Whoever. Maybe her ex.

BIXBY: She doesn't want him back.

RAVENEL: Even better: *conflict*!
However you wanta handle it, Bix.
But she needs to get laid.
On our watch.

(Title: RECURRENT*)*

(Image: CLAIRE's *apartment.)*

(On stage, CLAIRE *is sleeping. In the room with her,* [T V]
is on.)

> *(On a monitor: We see*
> CLAIRE, *in night-vision*
> *green, as she tosses and*
> *turns.)*

[T V]: You're in your
room, in the house

> *(On another monitor:*

where you grew up.
And you're afraid.

Dusk: fireflies are
coming out.
The house is quiet.
Are you alone in the
house?
Are your parents alive?
You can't remember.

The tide is out—you can
tell, by the smell.
But earlier—did you go
crabbing?
Slimy chicken-neck,
and a sinker,
end of a string—and
that net, with a hole...

Your mother's in bed—
she's Disappointed
Again—
your father's gone back
to Work,
where it's safe...
the house is quiet...

How long have the crabs
been out on the porch,
in that basket, under
your window?

Before, they were
scrabbling over each
other—
now you don't hear
anything...

we see a video of CLAIRE's
dream:)

(CLAIRE *is on a porch,
staring at an old table—on
top of which is a gleaming
black box.)*

*(The box is open, but we
can't see inside it.)*

(Reluctantly, CLAIRE
approaches the box.)

*(*CLAIRE's *P O V: The
ominous box is looming...)*

*(Is something moving
inside?)*
*(*CLAIRE's *arm moves into*

> *the frame—fearfully*
> *reaching into the box…)*

(CLAIRE, on stage, sits up with a gasp, waking from her nightmare.)

> *(The dream-monitor goes dark.)*

[T V]: Claire…
What are you hearing *now*?
Anything moving at all?

CLAIRE: Hello? Is someone…

(Pause)

[T V]: Claire…

(CLAIRE is too afraid to answer.)

[T V]: Tomorrow is the first treatment?

CLAIRE: Yes…

[T V]: Who's taking you [there]?
(Pause)
Who's holding your hand?
(Pause)
Who's bringing you home?

CLAIRE: A taxi…

[T V: How did you come to be so alone?

(CLAIRE lies back down—on stage, and on the night-vision monitor.)

(As CLAIRE drifts off, [T V] hums the theme from "Jeopardy", a lullaby.)

(Title: MAGIC BULLET)

(Image: DOCTOR's office.)

(CLAIRE is about to get her first treatment. CAMERAMAN is set up on the side.

(On another monitor, the CAMERAMAN's Live feed.)

DOCTOR: Are you nervous?

(CLAIRE *shakes her head, unconvincingly.*)

DOCTOR:Don't be nervous.

CLAIRE: Do you think—has that ever made anybody relax?
"Don't be nervous." "O K!"

(*Nervous himself, the* DOCTOR *hits intercom.*)

DOCTOR: We're still waiting for that delivery?

(*Intercom squawks.* DOCTOR *clarifies:*)

DOCTOR: Claire Forster's protocol.

(*Intercom squawks. To* CLAIRE:)

DOCTOR: It's on its way up from the pharmacy.
They had to log it into the data-base—

CLAIRE: You're talking…but I don't seem to be hearing anything you're saying.

DOCTOR: You can still change your mind—

CLAIRE: I can see your mouth is moving, it's odd, but—nothing.

(*Pause*)

DOCTOR: —or keep telling yourself—it worked in mice.

(CLAIRE *stares at* DOCTOR.)

CLAIRE: My question is, where do they find so many cancerous wee beasties?

DOCTOR: In a lab.
They're bred to have cancer.

(CLAIRE *is horrified, but covers.*)

CLAIRE: "Sucks to be you," I was saying to a mouse, just the other day…

(*A* NURSE *enters, with a prescription bottle she gives to the* DOCTOR.)

(NURSE *exits.* DOCTOR *checks the bottle, hands it to*
CLAIRE. *She opens it, shakes out a single capsule.*)

CLAIRE: It's a pill.

(*On the monitor, we zoom in on the pill resting in* CLAIRE's
sweaty palm.)

DOCTOR: You knew it would be a pill.

CLAIRE: But it doesn't seem—painful enough. To work.
Sharp needles—swollen bags of poison...
(*Pause*)
Maybe I *do* want death-rays
burning my skin. Down to the bone.

(DOCTOR *points to* CLAIRE's *hand that* isn't *clutching the
pill.*)

DOCTOR: Hold that hand above your head.

CLAIRE: Why?

DOCTOR: Because I'm telling you to.

(CLAIRE *obliges, painfully.*)

(*Camera pulls back, to take in this action.*)

CLAIRE: It hurts—

DOCTOR: I'm not done.
Now bend that arm, so your elbow is
slightly above your head.

(CLAIRE *tries.*)

CLAIRE: I don't think I—can...

DOCTOR: Like this.

(DOCTOR *wrenches* CLAIRE's *arm into place—she cries out.*)

DOCTOR: Now hold that position—while I go to
another, safer lead-lined room far away.
Don't *move!*
Or you'll blur the X-ray.
(*He watches her for a moment.*)

Is that real enough?
(He offers her a glass of water.)
Here.

(But CLAIRE *doesn't drop the painful position.)*

DOCTOR: What are you doing?

CLAIRE: Seeing how much I can stand.
(A stand-off. Finally, wincing, Claire drops her arm.)
Was I close?

DOCTOR: No. A session would last a lot longer.

CLAIRE: Then you think I made the right choice.

DOCTOR: Maybe hoping I could convince myself.

*(*CLAIRE *shoves her hand, with the pill in it, towards the* CAMERAMAN.*)*

CLAIRE: Are you getting this?
(She looks at the DOCTOR.*)*

(The pill in close-up, in CLAIRE's *open palm.)*

CLAIRE: Magic bullet.

DOCTOR: *(Still cautionary)*
Claire—…

CLAIRE: Targets just the bad guys.
Just the cancer. Not the rest of me.
(Shooting:)
Bam! Bam—bam—bam—bam—bam…
Not the lining of my anus—
or my hair, blowing out the car window—
or the inside of my mouth, ulcerating—
just those Cancerous Girls Gone Wild…

DOCTOR: The cancer cells are female?

CLAIRE: Females with humongous tits—
swarming up to the handsome cameraman
to shake their mutant ta-tas…
(To the DOCTOR:*)*

You don't believe in magic bullets—
do you?

DOCTOR: I don't believe in mutant ta-tas, either.

(Title: ONE-TAKE SHOT*)*

(Image: T V control room)

(On a monitor, CLAIRE *is about to take the pill.* BIXBY *and*
RAVENEL *watch.)*

BIXBY: What are you hoping will happen?

RAVENEL: When she takes the pill?

*(*BIXBY *nods.)*

RAVENEL: Her head explodes.

(Dumbfounded, BIXBY *turns off the monitor.)*

BIXBY: "Her head explodes."

RAVENEL: Were you watching, when New Orleans was
going under?

BIXBY: Yes.

RAVENEL: Did you want the levees to hold?

(Pause)

*(*BIXBY *turns the monitor back on.)*

(On screen: CLAIRE *swallows the pill, with a sip of water.)*

*(*BIXBY *and* RAVENEL *watch.)*

(Title: HALLOWEEN*)*

(Image: DOCTOR*'s office)*

*(*CLAIRE *has just taken the pill.)*

(On a monitor, we watch a live feed of CLAIRE*, who waits
for the drug to kick in.)*

CLAIRE: That's it?

DOCTOR: That's it.

CLAIRE: *(Only half-joking)*
Is it working?

DOCTOR: *(Ignoring)*
You'll need to be here for an hour,
while we monitor your vitals.

CLAIRE: Do you think I'll be able to tap-dance?

DOCTOR: Could you before?

(CLAIRE shakes her head.)

DOCTOR: Then probably not.
Is someone staying over, tonight?

CLAIRE: I couldn't find anybody.

(The DOCTOR isn't pleased.)

DOCTOR: Well, if you start to have a reaction—
anything—call. Don't wait.

CLAIRE: All right.
(Pause)
What kind of reaction?

DOCTOR: Anything: blurred vision, palpitations,
sweating,
headache or muscle aches, chills—

CLAIRE: My head explodes.

(Pause)

DOCTOR: Call me if your head explodes.
A nurse will be coming in.

*(DOCTOR exits. CLAIRE's alone on stage, waiting for
something to happen.)*

*(On the monitor, the live feed stops. Replacing the image, we
see a visual loop of one of Claire's fears: a pumpkin hits the
pavement, smashing to bits. Over and over.)*

(Title: 57,000 CHANNELS)

(Image: CLAIRE's apartment)

(CLAIRE *on the phone with her* MOTHER, *who shares the*
stage with CLAIRE.)

(On a monitor, a hidden cam is showing live feed of
CLAIRE—*alone—as she talks.)*

MOTHER: Can you believe I got Tivo?

CLAIRE: Mom—

MOTHER: So imagine—I'm ready to watch my stories,
Viki is Niki *again*—can you believe it?
that poor woman...
so I turn on the T V—and there you are.

CLAIRE: I was going to tell you...

MOTHER: Seriously?

CLAIRE: Ok, *no*—but I *thought* I should tell you...

MOTHER: That night-vision green. It was eerie, Claire.
Hard to make out, at first, what it was—
just a woman, tossing and turning...
took me awhile to realize—
it was you, in your bed, being spied on,
while you were sleeping—on T V.
(Pause)
My daughter—asleep in her lonely bed,
being spied on—by the whole world.

(Pause)

CLAIRE: How's Florida?

MOTHER: Like the waiting room for Hell.

CLAIRE: I thought you liked shuffleboard.

MOTHER: You push a thing with a stick.
It doesn't fill an entire day.

(Pause)

CLAIRE: I don't think you should watch the show.

MOTHER: How can I not? It's "must-see-T V".

CLAIRE: No—that's another network.
And "must-see-T V" was a very long time ago.
You *don't* have to see this, Mom.

MOTHER: Why are you doing this to me?

(Pause)

CLAIRE: Dying, you mean? Or becoming a star?

MOTHER: Oh god—

CLAIRE: Mom, that was a joke.
I'm not a star.
I'm not sure anyone else is watching the show—
except my mother.

(Pause)

MOTHER: I want to be with you.

CLAIRE: We talked about that.

MOTHER: Before you got sick.

CLAIRE: No.

MOTHER: I'm coming anyway.

CLAIRE: *No!*

MOTHER: Claire—

CLAIRE: *(Quoting)*
"My lonely bed."
You were watching me sleeping, on T V, in my "lonely
bed".
Mother, why would say that?
Why would you *see* that?
Yes, I'm alone!
No, I never remarried.
That's what happened! I'm sorry.
And yes, if you want to be with me, in my final hour—

MOTHER: Claire—don't—

CLAIRE:—you can check your local listings.
(Pause)
I had the first treatment today.
I'm taking this drug—that I couldn't get anywhere else.
That's why I'm on the show.
I think that episode airs on Friday.

MOTHER: You know I'm afraid of needles—

CLAIRE: This is a pill.

MOTHER: And that's the episode?
We watch you taking a pill?

CLAIRE: I know—but then it gets better.
I start to bleed from the eyes.
Then I turn purple, and my nose falls off.

(Pause)

MOTHER: You were purple when you came out of me.

(Pause)

CLAIRE: O K, you win—that was grosser than anything
I could've possibly thought you'd say.

MOTHER: You came out of me.
I know you regret that it was not some other womb.
But sadly for you, it was mine.
And you hurt like hell, coming out—

CLAIRE: But you're not bitter.

MOTHER: No—I forgave you.

(At that moment, CLAIRE is hit with a wave of pain.)

(She drops the phone, bites down on her hand, trying not to
scream.)

(Not knowing what's happened, MOTHER continues to talk.)

MOTHER: Or maybe it wasn't even forgiveness.
Maybe I just forgot the pain.
You wouldn't think that was possible.

But it has to be—or everyone
would be an only child.

(Out of nowhere, there's a knock at CLAIRE's *door.)*

*(*CLAIRE, *bent over in pain, looks up.)*

(Another monitor: The hallway outside CLAIRE's *apartment.*
BIXBY *stands at the door.)*

CLAIRE: Who is it?

BIXBY: *(On monitor)*
Ms Foster? It's Bixby Elliot…

MOTHER: Of course, *I* was an old child…

CLAIRE: It's eleven o'clock at—
what do you want?

BIXBY: It *is* late, and I'm sorry to bother you—
but I knew you had your first treatment—
and you were—
I mean, there was no-one—

CLAIRE: Yes! I'm *alone!*

MOTHER: Claire? You sound so far away.

BIXBY:—and I wanted to see if you were
all right.

CLAIRE: Mister Elliot? Why do you care?

MOTHER: I think we're breaking up—can you hear me?
(Pause.)
Sweetheart, can you hear me now?

*(*CLAIRE *picks up the phone, shuts it off—tosses it aside.)*

CLAIRE: In fact, I'm *not* alone—am I?
Aren't there—how many cameras—taking me in?
And I'm appearing now, in some control room,
on a monitor?

BIXBY: You are—but this is the night shift.
No one is watching.

(Pause)

I wasn't spying on you.

(CLAIRE *finds a pill-bottle, shakes out a tablet, dry-swallows.)*

CLAIRE: The guilty man fleeth—

BIXBY: —"where no one pursueth." O K.
Then I'll say good-night.

CLAIRE: I'm taking a pill, Mister Elliot—
(Shakes out another, dry-swallows.)
—no, I'm taking two. For the pain.
I'll be fine.

(Pause)

BIXBY: When you said you wanted to live
without hope—did that include the hope
that others would be concerned about
you?

(CLAIRE *doesn't answer.)*

(BIXBY *exits, walking out of camera range, disappearing
from the monitor.)*

(CLAIRE *stares at the bottle of pills. She shakes out another,
pops it.)*

(Title: COMRADE*)*

(Image: a hospital waiting-room)

(CLAIRE *sits next to a frail man,* CONTESTANT 2, *who keeps
eyeing her.)*

(On monitors, daytime T V is playing.)

CONTESTANT 2: Do I know you?

CLAIRE: Absolutely not.

CONTESTANT 2: You're on that show—*Final Battle.*

CLAIRE: I've been told that I look like that woman.
That's all.

CONTESTANT 2: *(Pointing off)*
That cameraman seems to think so.

CLAIRE: You watch that show?

CONTESTANT 2: I'm on it. There's *my* cameraman—
(Pointing) right there.

CONTESTANT 2: *(Getting it)*
You're the long-suffering guy—with a smile.

CONTESTANT 2: *(Smiling)*
You've seen my work.

CLAIRE: Just heard some things.

CONTESTANT 2: *(Surprised)*
You're not watching the show?

CLAIRE: I'm living the show.

CONTESTANT 2: Does your life make sense?

CLAIRE: No.

CONTESTANT 2: The show makes sense.
You might find it helpful.

CONTESTANT 2: They call you "the nice one".

CONTESTANT 2: Who does?

(CLAIRE points to the off-stage CAMERAMEN.)

CLAIRE: The crew.

CONTESTANT 2: I'm not—nice.
But I'm *playing* nice, on T V.
You need a persona.

CLAIRE: Who told you that?

CONTESTANT 2: I read a book—how to make it big, on
Reality Television.

(CLAIRE doesn't respond.)

(CONTESTANT 2 pulls out a deck of cards.)

CONTESTANT 2: So how are you doing?

(CLAIRE *doesn't answer.* CONTESTANT 2 *offers her the fanned-out deck.)*

CONTESTANT 2: Pick a card—any card.

(Reluctantly, CLAIRE *does so.)*

CONTESTANT 2: Make sure you remember what it was. Now slide it back into the deck.

(CLAIRE *does.* CONTESTANT 2 *awkwardly shuffles.)*

(Then he fans out the deck, face up, till he comes to a card.)

CONTESTANT 2: Was it the ace of Spades?

CLAIRE: No.

(CONTESTANT 2's *taken aback, but tries again.)*

CONTESTANT 2: Was it the ten of Clubs?

CLAIRE: No.

CONTESTANT 2: *(A little more desperate)* King of Clubs.

CLAIRE: Nuh-uh.

CONTESTANT 2: Three of hearts.

CLAIRE: No.

CONTESTANT 2: Jack of Diamonds.

CLAIRE: No.
(Pause)
Sorry.

(Pause. CONTESTANT 2 *regards* CLAIRE.)

CONTESTANT 2: How *are* you doing?

CLAIRE: Better than you.

CONTESTANT 2: You think the cancer's spread to my brain.

(CLAIRE's *silent.)*

CONTESTANT 2: You're not walking as well as you were,
in last night's episode.

CLAIRE: Thank you for noticing.

(Pause. CONTESTANT 2 *surveys the room.)*

CONTESTANT 2: All the people in this waiting-room…
sometimes you get to wondering:
does *everyone* have cancer?

CLAIRE: This is why I fast-forward.
(Using a walker, she gets to her feet, starts to move off.)

CONTESTANT 2: I read about you, in a gossip rag.
You live alone. You won't let anyone help you.
How is that working out?

NURSE *(O S)* Claire Forster?

CLAIRE: It *was* the ace of Spades.

CONTESTANT 2: Then why—

CLAIRE:—to see you squirm.
Fuck you.

*(*CLAIRE *exits—and her* CAMERAMAN *now appears, as he follows her off.)*

(Still being filmed by his cameraman, CONTESTANT 2 *looks out.)*

CONTESTANT 2: All these people…
(He starts to count heads.)
You, and you, and you, and—maybe not you—
but you, and you…

(Title: …AND I CAN'T GET UP)

(Image: CLAIRE's *apartment)*

([T V] in the background, silent.)

*(*CLAIRE *is awkwardly pacing,   (On a monitor, we get a live
bringing her walker down   feed from a hidden*

hard, like she was planting   *apartment-cam, of*
a flag on a war-torn beach: C*LAIRE as she paces,*
...thump—, thump—,   *moving in and out of*
thump—, thump—   *camera range.*

(She's waiting for a magic transformation she knows isn't coming that night—or maybe ever.)

(Thump—thump—thump—thump...up and down the apartment.)

(Her cell-phone rings. She stops to answer.)

CLAIRE: Hello?
(...)
Oh, I'm sorry, Mrs. Lipschitz.
I didn't realize—
(...)
No, it isn't a pogo stick.
It's a walker—
(...)
a *walker*, but I'll keep it down.
(...)
No, not bursitis...
(...)
[Well] I'm sorry, that must be painful.
(...)
A vale of *what*?
(...)
Oh *yes*, it is that...
(...)
Well, try to get back to sleep, Mrs Lipschitz—
(...)
I *know*, at your age it's hard, but try—
(...)
That's right, and no more pogo stick.
(She hangs up.)
You cow. You ignorant slut.
(She starts to pace again, slower and more quietly.)

(Then she stops, wondering if…)
(She lets go of the walker, tests her balance.)
(Then she steps away from the walker, trying to take a few steps on her own.)
(So far, so good. She takes a few steps more—is this getting easier?)
(Now she's fighting a sense of what has to be premature elation.)
(Addressing the room)
Ladies and gentlemen…
I can walk without my walker…
(She keeps pacing.)
I can walk without my walker!
(She starts to walk in a circle, slightly faster, slightly more confident.)
(Suddenly there's a spasm of pain—one of her legs gives out—and she falls to the floor.)
(She lies there stunned—not even crying or cursing.)

*(The cell-phone starts to ring again—*CLAIRE *lets it ring till it stops.)*

(Monitor freezes: on the image of CLAIRE *lying helpless, on the floor.)*

[T V]: Previously, on *Final Battle*…
(As CLAIRE*)*
Ladies and gentlemen…
I can walk without my walker…
I can walk without my walker!
(She falls to the floor, as CLAIRE *did.)*
(Pause)
Claire…

CLAIRE: What?

[T V]: Claire…
Do you think the drug is working?
(Title: I'VE FALLEN DOWN…*)*

(Image: BIXBY'*s apartment)*

*(*BIXBY, *in his bathrobe, watches tonight's episode of* Final Battle.*)*

(On a monitor, the moment we just saw: CLAIRE *falling down.)*

(Softly, in the background, Ride of the Valkyrie *is playing.)*

*(*BIXBY *stares at the image of* CLAIRE, *in pain, on the floor.)*

WOMAN: *(O S)*
Bix?
Come back to bed.
I'm lonely…

BIXBY: *(Shouting)*
So am I!

(Pause)

WOMAN: *(O S, puzzled)*
What?

(Title: VAST WASTELAND*)*

(Image: RAVENEL'*s office.)*

*(*RAVENEL *is watching a monitor.)*

(On the monitor: live feed of BIXBY *in his living room.)*

*(*RAVENEL *watches* BIXBY *watching* CLAIRE *on the floor.)*

RAVENEL: Impossible obsession—check.
Unprofessional behavior—nice.
Queasy sex and the shadow of death:
do I smell Emmy?

END OF ACT ONE

ACT TWO

(Title: SPOON*)*

(Image: CLAIRE'*s apartment)*

(It's empty for the moment, except for [T V].*)*

(On a monitor, a frozen image of CLAIRE *and an E R* DOCTOR.*)*

[T V]: *(As* E R DOC*)*
It's not serious, Miss Forster—
(As CLAIRE*)*
But I can't even stand up straight,
the pain is so bad—
(As E R DOC*)*
Last time you had a bowel movement was…?
(As CLAIRE*)*
What?
(As E R DOC*)*
When's the last time you moved your bowels?
(As CLAIRE*)*
I don't—remember—why??
(As E R DOC*)*
The x-rays all look fine, except that you're badly constipated.
(As CLAIRE*)*
I'm doubled over…because I am full of shit.
(As E R DOC*)*
That's the story.
Could be a side-effect of the new medication.

Anyway, here.
(She takes an object offered by the doctor.)
(As CLAIRE*)*
What's this?
(As E R DOC*)*
You need to dig yourself out.
(As CLAIRE*)*
With a spoon?
(As E R DOC*)*
There's a bathroom, right over there.
(As CLAIRE*)*
By myself…
(As E R DOC*)*
The E R's busy tonight. Look around.
(As CLAIRE*)*
I'm in terrible pain—I'm all alone—
and you want me to shove a spoon up my ass—
(As E R DOC*)*
Just do it, and it'll be over.

(Now the taped action continues, on the monitor that had been showing the frozen image of CLAIRE *and the* E R DOC*.)*

(We're in a corridor right outside the E R—tracking the bent-over CLAIRE *as she makes her way, with her walker, to a bathroom.)*

(At the bathroom door, CLAIRE *turns to face the camera.)*

CLAIRE: *(On monitor)*
What are you doing?

*(*CAMERAMAN *[O C} mumbles something inaudible.)*

CLAIRE: Are you kidding me?
You can't go in there!

*(*CAMERAMAN *[O C] inaudible)*

CLAIRE: No!
Get the hell away from me!

(Onscreen, CLAIRE hobbles into the bathroom, disappearing from view as she frantically closes the door.)

(On stage, CLAIRE enters her living room, in her hand, a glass dessert-cup of chocolate pudding. Nibbling on her dessert with a spoon, she takes a look up at the T V screen.)

(On the monitor, we see the camera moving up to the bathroom door. Now we can hear sounds: groans, cries of pain.)

CLAIRE: *(O C, faint)*
Oh god...oh jesus...

(Horrified, CLAIRE listens to herself—in the past—wrestling with the spoon.)

(Title: TINO)

(BIXBY's drinking, watching a baseball replay game on the big T V above the bar.)

(CLAIRE approaches BIXBY, using a cane, a drink in her other hand.)

CLAIRE: Come here often?

BIXBY: *(Startled)*
Claire!

CLAIRE: What's your sign? Mine is Cancer.
Huh...
You know how you start to say something,
thinking it *might* be funny—*maybe*—
but probably not, it's probably stupid—
and then you blurt it out anyway?
And you were right? It's astoundingly dumb—
and your friends are embarrassed *for* you?
"What's your sign?" "Tumor..." D'oh...

(Pause)

BIXBY: Are you following me?

CLAIRE: Yes.

(Pause)

BIXBY: Look, I'm sorry—

CLAIRE: About?

BIXBY: I don't know—you tell me.
(Pause)
Are you supposed to be drinking?
While you're on the new medication?

CLAIRE: Are you supposed to be filming me,
when I'm on my hands and knees in a bathroom,
digging out my painfully bulging rectum with a
spoon?

BIXBY: At least…

CLAIRE: What?

BIXBY: Nothing.

CLAIRE: *What?*

BIXBY: We didn't push open the door.
(Pause)
That would be one of those things I started to say—
and shouldn't have said.

(Pause)

*(*CLAIRE *is looking at the* [T V] *screen.)*

CLAIRE: I used to fantasize about Tino Martinez.

(Off BIXBY's *puzzled look,* CLAIRE *nods at the face on the screen.)*

CLAIRE: Tino Martinez.
What year is this game—'98? 99?
In the Baseball Season Time Forgot—
when the Yankees didn't suck…
I liked it, when he hit a home run—
because, when he'd made it all the way home,
he'd take off his cap, to salute the fans…
and he had the most beautiful head of hair…

BIXBY: Were you married, then?
I just wondered...if you husband knew...

CLAIRE: When he was pinch-hitting for Tino...?
I never told him.
(Pause)
So maybe Tino Martinez is watching *Final Battle.*
It's possible, right?
And he's there, with the cameraman,
and the rest of the audience,
in that hallway...
Tino Martinez, the Man of my Dreams.
What is Tino seeing in his head, behind Door Number
Two?

(Pause)
The camera should have gone in.
Could it be worse than what people imagined?

BIXBY: I'm sorry.

CLAIRE: Like the monster, in a horror film,
when you finally see it: oh.

BIXBY: You like horror movies.

CLAIRE: Yes. They've started to feel like documentaries.

BIXBY: Zombies?

CLAIRE: No so much.

BIXBY: Same here. I'm not afraid of the dead.
I'm afraid of the living.

CLAIRE: I know what you mean. Let's fuck.

(BIXBY's taken aback, tries to cover.)

BIXBY: I'm seeing someone.

CLAIRE: I'm riddled with cancer. Your guilt would be
finite.

BIXBY: I'm Jewish. Guilt is forever.

CLAIRE: I know what you mean.
So yes? A quick one?
In and out? Easy come, easy go?

(Calling CLAIRE*'s bluff—and surprising herself—*BIXBY
*pulls her close and kisses her, hard. She doesn't fight him,
but doesn't kiss back.)*

BIXBY: You didn't want that.

CLAIRE: I guess I'm still sober.

BIXBY: Music to a guy's ears...

CLAIRE: If you loan me two tens, I can have another
twenty-dollar martini.

BIXBY: Why are you following me?

*(*CLAIRE *doesn't respond.)*

(Title: CLOSING THE DEAL*)*

(Image: RAVENEL*'s office)*

(On another monitor: live feed of BIXBY *and* CLAIRE*, at the
bar.)*

*(*RAVENEL *is watching the monitor, incensed.)*

RAVENEL: You *faggot.*
(Pause)
Bixby...
(Pause)
Close the fucking *deal.*
I love you like a father, but—
(He suddenly feels a stab of pain in his chest.)
—goddamit, you are killing me—
*(He fumbles in his pocket, pulls out a pill-box. In his agony,
he drops the box, pills scatter.)*
No...—SHIT...
(He sinks to his knees, grabs a pill, pops it under his tongue.)
*(The pain subsides. Shaken, he eases into sitting on the
floor.)*
(Composed enough, he looks back at the monitor.)

(On the monitor, CLAIRE *has begun to unbutton her blouse.)*

*(*BIXBY *looks uneasy.)*

*(*CLAIRE *takes one of* BIXBY'S *hands, puts it inside her blouse.)*

*(*RAVENEL *watches, astonished. He starts to laugh.)*

RAVENEL: That's my boy…

Title: MY HUMPS, MY HUMPS

(We're back in the bar. [T V] is standing in for the bar's T V.)

[T V]: Previously, on *Final Battle*…
(As BIXBY*)*
You didn't want that.
(As CLAIRE*)*
I guess I'm still sober.
(As Bixby)
Music to a guy's ears…
(As CLAIRE*)*
If you loan me two tens, I can buy another twenty-dollar martini.

(At this point, BIXBY and CLAIRE resume their scene.

BIXBY: Why are you following me?

*(*CLAIRE *starts to unbutton her blouse.)*

CLAIRE: I want to show you something…

BIXBY: Claire…

*(*CLAIRE *takes one of his hands, puts it inside her blouse.)*

CLAIRE: Just above my breast—near the armpit— can you feel it?

BIXBY: We're in a public place—

CLAIRE: *(Dismissing)*
We're young—well, "ish",
we're in love—

BIXBY: We're being filmed.

CLAIRE: *(First hesitation)*
I ducked out on my cameraman.

BIXBY: There's more than one.

(BIXBY *tries to withdraw his hand,* CLAIRE *holds it firmly in place.)*

CLAIRE: *(Looking around)*
Where?

BIXBY: I don't know—could be any one of them.
That sketchy guy in the bowling shirt…
I think—is he aiming his gym bag at us?

CLAIRE: Why are you telling me *now*?

BIXBY: Because—due to circumstances beyond my control—
I seem to be—groping you…

CLAIRE: Does it matter?
Won't they blur your face?

BIXBY: It isn't me I'm worried about.

(Pause. CLAIRE *plunges on, moving* BIXBY's *hand.)*

CLAIRE: Can you feel it?

BIXBY: What?

CLAIRE: A lump—above my breast,
on the edge of my armpit.

BIXBY: I can feel—something. There?

CLAIRE: Yes.
One of the metastases.
(Pause)
I think it's smaller.

BIXBY: Is it?

CLAIRE: I think the treatment is working.

BIXBY: What do the doctors say?

CLAIRE: I'm having a body scan tomorrow.
(Pause)
I think the drug is working.
I could live.
How can I live with that?

(BIXBY gently withdraws his hand.)

CLAIRE: Everything I've done with my life has been wrong.
I'd have to start over again.
(Pause)
Come home with me.

BIXBY: I can't—
be a part of your story.

CLAIRE: You already are.

(CLAIRE kisses BIXBY—he hesitates.)

CLAIRE: My breath is bad—

BIXBY: No.

CLAIRE: I'm rotting inside.

BIXBY: *(Moving closer)*
Do not talk dirty to me.

CLAIRE: You have a *terrible* job.

BIXBY: I do. And this is completely impossible.

(BIXBY and CLAIRE kiss again, this time with some real heat.)

[T V]: Martinez *hammered* that ball—
that ball is outa here, gone, goodbye!

(Title: RECURRENT [2])

(Image: CLAIRE's apartment)

(On stage, CLAIRE and BIXBY lie in each other's arms, asleep.)

(On a monitor: We see the two, in night-vision green, entwined.)

(On another monitor: We see a video of CLAIRE's *dream: she is on the porch again, starring at the sinister gleaming black box atop the old table. Reluctantly, she approaches the box. As she does so, crabs come boiling over the edge of the box, dropping onto the table top and clattering onto the porch. Frightened, she takes a step back from the waving claws. The image freezes.)*

(On stage, CLAIRE *moans.* BIXBY *wakes, sees that she's dreaming.)*

BIXBY: Claire?

*(*CLAIRE *wakes, with a start.)*

CLAIRE: What—…

BIXBY: It was just a bad dream.

CLAIRE: Oh.

BIXBY: You O K?

CLAIRE: I don't know.

BIXBY: Go back to sleep.

*(*BIXBY *and* CLAIRE *settle back into a spoon, with him curled around her.)*

*(*CLAIRE *moves his hand again to her breast.)*

CLAIRE: It's smaller than it was…

BIXBY: Lady, give me a *moment—*

CLAIRE: Not *your* lump…

BIXBY: Oh…

*(*CLAIRE *starts to laugh—a sleepy laugh.)*

*(*BIXBY *laughs too. They settle again.)*

BIXBY: It's smaller than it was…

(On the monitor: We hold on the image of CLAIRE *and the crabs.)*

(Title: HOCUS POCUS)

(Image: hospital waiting room)

*(*CLAIRE *sits between* FEMALE PATIENT—*who's wearing a turban, to cover her baldness—and* CONTESTANT 2. *He tries to catch her eye, but she won't look at him.)*

FEMALE PATIENT: Terrible.

CLAIRE: What?

FEMALE PATIENT: To be your own evil twin.

(Off CLAIRE's *puzzled look,* FEMALE PATIENT *points at the television.)*

FEMALE PATIENT: Viki is Niki again.
Poor woman.

CLAIRE: Ah.

FEMALE PATIENT: They keep thinking she's cured.

CLAIRE: What would be the fun in that?

(Nodding, the FEMALE PATIENT *resumes her watching.)*

*(*CONTESTANT 2 *takes advantage of the silence.)*

CONTESTANT 2: *(To* CLAIRE)
So how are you doing?

CLAIRE: How are you?

CONTESTANT 2: Whatever I'm on—it's not working.
So I'm off the show. They're starting me
on radiation tomorrow.

CLAIRE: Can you go like this?

*(*CLAIRE *demonstrates one of the painful positions—arm above her head—that the* DOCTOR *had put her through. She winces.)*

*(*CONTESTANT 2 *tries to imitate, can't.)*

CONTESTANT 2: *(Winded)*
Uh-uh.

CLAIRE: Then good luck.

(CONTESTANT 2 *grits his teeth, rides out a wave of pain.*)

CONTESTANT 2: Have you fallen in love yet?

CLAIRE: No.

CONTESTANT 2: They must be behind schedule.

CLAIRE: What are you talking about?

CONTESTANT 2: I was in the producer's office,
signing all the papers I had to sign,
so they could kick a dying man off the show—
and I found your storyline.

CLAIRE: My what?

(CONTESTANT 2 *pulls out a xeroxed paper.*)

(CLAIRE *grabs for it—he jerks it away.*)

CLAIRE: I fall in love?

(CONTESTANT 2 *nods.*)

CLAIRE: And then what?
How does it end?

CONTESTANT 2: Now you see it…
*(He starts ripping the paper up, into smaller and smaller
bits.)*

FEMALE PATIENT: *(Watching T V)*
My mother useta say,
I had the devil in me.
I believed her.
I didn't need an evil twin.

(CONTESTANT 2 *tosses his confetti into the air.*)

CONTESTANT 2: … now you don't.

NURSE: *(O S)*
Thomas James?

(CONTESTANT 2 *gets up and exits.*)

(CLAIRE *starts to pick up the confetti—then realizes it's hopeless. She scatters the scraps again.*)

(*For a moment she sits, unable to move.*)

FEMALE PATIENT: (*Pointing out the T V*)
He useta have a scar—that one?
But that was a couple of actors ago.

(*As the* FEMALE PATIENT *talks,* CLAIRE *takes an eyebrow pencil from her purse.*)

(*She begins to draw mouse-whiskers on her face.*)

FEMALE PATIENT: At first, he was just a date-rapist.
But he was popular—fans would mob him,
they'd be screaming, "Todd, rape me! Rape me!"
Now, turns out he's Viki's half-brother, somehow.
I did *not* see *that* coming…

(*As a commercial comes on,* FEMALE PATIENT *notices* CLAIRE *making up.*)

FEMALE PATIENT: Honey, you ok?

CLAIRE: Do I look like a mouse?

FEMALE PATIENT: You don't have the ears.

NURSE (*O S*)
Claire Forster?

(*Title:* A BETTER MOUSETRAP [THWACK]*)

(*Image:* DOCTOR'*s office*)

(DOCTOR'*s reading the lab results in* CLAIRE'*s file, ignoring her get-up—she still has the painted on-whiskers, and she's also darkened the tip of her nose.*)

DOCTOR: Well, the primary tumor hasn't shrunk—
but it hasn't gotten larger.
Two of the metastatic lesions *are* smaller.
One has disappeared.

CLAIRE: Disappeared?

DOCTOR: According to the scan.

CLAIRE: That's—amazing. Isn't it?

DOCTOR: It's better than we expected.

CLAIRE: All right…

DOCTOR: So that's the good news, Claire…

CLAIRE: And the bad news is…

DOCTOR: You're turning into a mouse.

CLAIRE: Or I was always a mouse—
whaddya think?
Isn't that what happens?
You turn into what you already were?
There was a story line we were following.
I was supposed to fall in love.
I don't know if I died or not—
maybe they had two different endings:
I lived, and we got married
and finally children were running around *everywhere*.
Or, [B], the cancer returned—
but he made me strong—my *man*—
and I died a good death—

DOCTOR: No, that wouldn't work.

CLAIRE: Why not?

DOCTOR: Because there is no "good death". Sorry.
"Dying with dignity" is a myth.
For most of us, it's painful and it's degrading.
And we lose everything.

(Pause)

CLAIRE: Who *are* you?
I don't like you.
How did you end up being a doctor?

DOCTOR: I wanted to make a *lot* of money.

CLAIRE: Aha! You pretend to joke—but you're not.

DOCTOR: And along the way, I wanted to help a few people.

CLAIRE: Did you?

DOCTOR: I don't know.
(Pause)
They all die, sooner or later.
Which is bothersome, when you think of it.

CLAIRE: Maybe that's why the Rolex, and the fancy car and the trophy wife: to distract you from the fact that you keep losing. Over and over.

(Titlle: MONEY SHOT)

(Image: RAVENEL's office)

(RAVENEL is watching a monitor.)

(On the monitor: Taped night-vision of BIXBY and CLAIRE making love.)

(BIXBY enters. He joins RAVENEL in watching, for a moment.)

RAVENEL: *(Of BIXBY on screen)*
You've been working out.
You look good.

BIXBY: I'm vain.

RAVENEL: Enjoy it while you can.
(Pause)
She's beautiful.

BIXBY: Do you think so? We look—

RAVENEL: In this light…

BIXBY: —like we're decomposing.

RAVENEL: Oh yeah, *that's* hot.

BIXBY: You wanted X-rated…?

RAVENEL: Something like. It could've been.
But the angle is bad.
And you don't know how to fuck.

(BIXBY *and* RAVENEL *watch, for a moment.*)

BIXBY: I know how to fuck.
Christ.

RAVENEL: A little *heat*—that's asking too much?
You look like you're playing Twister.

BIXBY: I was hurting her.
Whatever I did—however I moved—I was hurting her.
She couldn't find a position where she was
comfortable—
where she wasn't in pain.

RAVENEL: Why didn't you stop?

BIXBY: Because she wanted to come.
(*Pause*)
You don't remember anything, when you're coming.
That's what she wanted.

(BIXBY *and* RAVENEL *watch.* RAVENEL *points at the screen.*)

RAVENEL: Is she coming now?

BIXBY: I never knew, exactly—when it—was.
I was thinking too much:
"I don't want to hurt you.
Oh god, I do not want to hurt you…"

RAVENEL: That's why you're a lousy fuck.
You're considerate. It's a turn-off.

BIXBY: She has a tumor pressing against her spine—

RAVENEL: You know what? *Fuck* the tumor!
I have angina.
FUCK THE ANGINA!
And *you*—fuck you! Why don't you fucking *live*?

(*Pause*)

BIXBY: I didn't know…

RAVENEL: No shit. I don't need you to bludgeon me
with your pity.
Are we clear on that?

(BIXBY *looks at the screen again, with increasing unease.*)

BIXBY: She said, at the very beginning—
she wanted to live without hope.

RAVENEL: I remember.

BIXBY: Do you think she made it?

RAVENEL: I don't know.

BIXBY: Have you?

RAVENEL: No.
I still want things.
(Pause)
So do you.

(BIXBY *aqnd* RAVENEL *stare at the screen.*)

RAVENEL: Like that assignment you had, as a kid:
"What I want to be, when I grow up…"
"I want to be a writer," you said,
"and make a lot of money."

BIXBY: I told you that?

RAVENEL: You drink too much.

BIXBY: I was nine. "A writer."
(Pause)
Jesus.

RAVENEL: Thwack.

BIXBY: Do you have to air this episode?

RAVENEL: Don't worry about it—we're superimposing
a Smiley Face on your head.
(Pause. He indicates the screen.)

You don't like this?
You wrote it.

(Not knowing how to respond, BIXBY *exits.)*

*(*RAVENEL *watches the lovers on screen, in the eerie night-vision light.)*

RAVENEL: That's my boy.
My beautiful boy…

(Title: KILL SWITCH

(Image: CLAIRE's *apartment/*RAVENEL's *office)*

*(*BIXBY *is sleeping.)*

(Quietly, trying not to wake him, CLAIRE *is packing a bag.)*

([T V] *watches* CLAIRE*.)*

[T V]: What are you doing?

*(*CLAIRE *ignores the voice.)*

[T V]: Claire…

*(*CLAIRE *keeps packing.)*

[T V]: You're tired. Go back to sleep.

CLAIRE: I don't like to take naps, anymore.

[T V]: Why not?

CLAIRE: Then I have to wake up twice—in one day.

[T V]: Is waking up so terrible?

CLAIRE: Waking is when I remember…

[T V]: What?

CLAIRE: That I'm afraid.

[T V]: Afraid of what?

CLAIRE: Not knowing—what will happen…

[T V]: Did you ever know?
You only thought you did.

CLAIRE: For the rest of my...—won't I be waiting for
the cancer to return?
I'm damaged. For the rest of my life.

[T V]: Maybe you'll get hit by a bus.

(Pause)

CLAIRE: Why is always a *bus*?

[T V]: Why are you always running away?

(CLAIRE registers [T V]'s challenge.)

BIXBY: *(Stirring)*
Claire? Are you on the phone?

CLAIRE: No...

BIXBY: Is the TV on? I heard voices...

[T V]: *(To CLAIRE)*
I'm not your friend.
I never was.

(CLAIRE nods.)

[T V]: I distract you. On occasion.

(CLAIRE exits briefly, returns with a shotgun.)

(She shoots [T V].)

([T V] explodes.)

*(All the monitors blaze to life in close-ups of geysers of blood.
Then they quickly fade to black.)*

(BIXBY—totally freaked—stumbles out of bed).

CLAIRE: I think I may be having some kind of
reaction to the drug...

BIXBY: You shot the T V.

CLAIRE: "... but I did not shoot the -"

BIXBY: Claire—you shot the *T V*.

CLAIRE: I know. Go home.

BIXBY: I'm calling your doctor.

CLAIRE: I'm holding a shotgun.
Maybe you should go.
Or isn't that part of the story?

(Title: ...NOW YOU DON'T)

(Images: CLAIRE's apartment/BIXBY's office.)

(RAVENEL watches BIXBY and CLAIRE on a monitor.)

(Continuous)

BIXBY: *(Playing a desperate game of catch-up)*
O K—you're right. I admit:
there was a story.

CLAIRE: A story *you* wrote.

BIXBY: But it changed.
It changed, because—
when I wrote the story—
(He pauses.)

CLAIRE: What?

BIXBY: I didn't know you were real.

(CLAIRE doesn't respond.)

BIXBY: Where are you going?

CLAIRE: I don't know.

BIXBY: Do you have any money?

CLAIRE: Not a lot.

BIXBY: How will you live?

CLAIRE: I can max out a couple of credit cards.

(Pause)

BIXBY: And then?
(Pause)
How will your doctor reach you?

(CLAIRE ignores BIXBY.)

BIXBY: Are you in pain?

CLAIRE: I have to go—

BIXBY: *(Quickly)*
Don't go.
(Pause)
Please don't go.

(BIXBY's phone starts ringing. By habit, he answers it.)

BIXBY: *What?*

RAVENEL: Let her storm off into the night.

BIXBY: WHAT?

RAVENEL: It'll make a terrific episode.
Very Gothic, very "freaked-out woman running from the castle…"

(BIXBY looks around, stunned, forgetting the phone in his hand.)

CLAIRE: What are you looking for?

BIXBY: There's a camera you didn't find.

(Now CLAIRE looks around too.)

CLAIRE: You're watching me now?
(She whirls around, looking for the invisible intruder.)
Are you?
Do you ever plan to stop fucking me?
(She starts to search for the camera.)

BIXBY: He wants you to run.

RAVENEL: In a night-gown, maybe—
barefoot—into a soaking rain—

(BIXBY, hearing RAVENEL's voice on the line, hangs up.)

RAVENEL: But you have to stay.
There are other drugs you haven't tried, yet—
chemo—radiation—

you can't—give up—
not now—

CLAIRE: The drug is working!

(BIXBY *is startled*.)

CLAIRE: And I'm terrified.
(Pause)
Everything I've done with my life has been wrong.
I see that, now.
I never knew what I should be, when I grew up.
So I worked at meaningless jobs.
I'd go home at night—
I'd go home at night…
Junk mail. Into the garbage.
Check the machine, out of habit:
no messages…
I don't want my mother near me.
I'm divorced.
And my friends have scattered…
Somehow, while my back was turned—
my world was getting smaller…
I'd go home at night.
I'd watch T V…
I did something wrong.
I was already dead—before my diagnosis.
Before I ever felt that pain in my back.
I never lived.
I'd go home at night…
I'd lie down on my bed…
…and I'd always be so glad that the day was over…
one more gone…

(Pause)

BIXBY: It happens…
People—find themselves alone—
and that's not what they wanted…

CLAIRE: And then they get sick.
And they look at the clock,
and it's late.
It's very late in the day.
(Pause)
Just enough time for a little T V, before bed.

BIXBY: You *shot* the T V.

(Pause)

CLAIRE: I don't know you at all.
I don't know what you want.
We slept together a couple of times...

(Pause)

BIXBY: Was it good for you?

CLAIRE: You're an idiot.
(She laughs, in spite of herself—and winces.)
Fuck—don't make me laugh—
it only hurts when I...
(Riding the pain)
jesus...

BIXBY: If the drug is working...

CLAIRE: It hasn't shrunk the main tumor, yet.
It's still pressing against my spine.

BIXBY: What can that feel like?

CLAIRE: What do you think?

(BIXBY tries to show her that he finally understands.)

BIXBY: You lived—you never knew why.
You put one foot in front of the other.
You thought, some day you'd figure it out—
some day that never came.
Then you got sick. And that was a whole new
way of getting lost:
you were drugged out, all the time,
or in constant pain...

There was nothing to figure out, anymore
You were just a body.

(Pause)

CLAIRE: Do you get how little that has to do
with what you put on the air?

(Watching CLAIRE, BIXBY *takes out his phone, calls*
RAVENEL.)

RAVENEL: This is golden—all of it—

BIXBY: Ravenel—I quit.

*(*CLAIRE *looks up at* BIXBY.)*

RAVENEL: O K, that'll be a nice moment—

BIXBY: I'm serious.

RAVENEL: Even better.

BIXBY: I'll clear out my desk on Monday.

RAVENEL: Don't you realize you're too late?

*(*BIXBY *is chilled, afraid that* RAVENEL's *right. He sees*
CLAIRE *looking off.)*

BIXBY: *(To* CLAIRE)
What are you looking at?

(Both BIXBY *and* CLAIRE *give the room another look.)*

CLAIRE: Is the camera in my copy of *Atlas Shrugged*?

RAVENEL: *(In his office, watching)*
No! *Fuck* no!

BIXBY: *("it's possible")*
If they needed a book that had been there forever—
that you would never touch...

*(*RAVENEL *shouts into the phone, which* BIXBY *hasn't hung
up.)*

RAVENEL: Tell her to read the fine print!

(Hearing RAVENEL *bellowing,* CLAIRE *takes the phone from*
BIXBY.*)*

CLAIRE: Tell me *what?*

RAVENEL: You think I don't care if you live or die.
Not true. You croak on camera,
our ratings would go through the roof.
So go ahead—run.
We'll track you down.
And when you're too weak to fight us off,
we'll shoot your final hours.

(Pause)

CLAIRE: What are you so afraid of, Mister Ravenel?
Are *you* dying?

*(*RAVENEL *is jolted.* CLAIRE *turns off the phone, hands it to*
BIXBY.*)*

BIXBY: Well—I'm out of a job.
I resigned—

CLAIRE: I know—on camera.

*(*CLAIRE *moves even closer, to kiss* BIXBY *goodbye—regretful*
but with tenderness.)

(Then, bag in hand, she heads for the bookshelf—and the
camera.)

BIXBY: Claire—
please…

(On the monitors, CLAIRE's *image gets larger, as she*
approaches the hidden camera. RAVENEL *watches her,*
mesmerized.)

*(*CLAIRE's hand reaches out, filling the screen.

CLAIRE: *(On monitor)*
Shh…
It'll be all right.
Now you see me…

(The camera-feed cuts off—all the screens in RAVENEL'*s office go blank.)*

*(*CLAIRE *exits.)*

*(*RAVENEL *stares at the empty screens.)*

*(*BIXBY *looks around the empty apartment. He hears the quiet click of a door, as it closes.)*

(Black-out)

END OF PLAY.

www.ingramcontent.com/pod-product-compliance
Lightning Source LLC
Chambersburg PA
CBHW052211090426
42741CB00010B/2498

* 9 7 8 0 8 8 1 4 5 6 5 0 9 *